READING POWER

Derek Jeter
Baseball's Best
Heather Feldman

The Rosen Publishing Group's
PowerKids Press ™
New York

1

For Sophie Megan

Published in 2001 by The Rosen Publishing Group, Inc.
29 East 21st Street, New York, NY 10010

First Edition

Book Design: Michael de Guzman

Photo Credits: pp. 5, 15 © AL BELLO/ALLSPORT; pp. 7, 19, 21 © EZRO SHAW/ALLSPORT; pp. 9, 11 SETH POPPEL YEARBOOK ARCHIVES; p. 13 © JAMIE SQUIRE/ ALLSPORT; p. 17 © OTTO GREULE/ALLSPORT.

Feldman, Heather.
    Derek Jeter : baseball's best / Heather Feldman.—1st ed.
      p. cm— (Reading power)
    Includes bibliographical references and index.
    Summary: A simple biography of the talented New York Yankees shortstop, discussing his popularity and three World Championships.
    ISBN 0-8239-5719-5 (alk. paper)
      1. Jeter, Derek, 1974—Juvenile literature. 2. Baseball players—United States—Biography—Juvenile literature. [1. Jeter, Derek, 1974- 2. Baseball players] I. Title. II. Series.

GV865.J48 F45 2000
796.357'092—dc21
[B]   00-028007

Manufactured in the United States of America

Contents

Derek Jeter is a great baseball player.

5

Derek plays shortstop. He plays shortstop for the New York Yankees.

7

In high school, Derek played baseball for his high school team.

Derek also played basketball in high school. He liked baseball better, though.

Derek catches a baseball that flies through the air.

13

Derek hits a baseball with his bat. Derek hits home runs.

15

Derek runs around the bases. He runs fast.

17

Derek and his teammates are happy when they win games. In 1999, Derek and the Yankees won the World Series.

19

Derek has many fans. His fans ask him to sign autographs for them. Derek is loved by many people.

Glossary

autograph (AW-toh-graf) A person's signature.

bases (BAY-sez) Four spots on the baseball field that players run to on their way to score a run. The bases are first, second, third, and home.

bat (BAT) What a baseball player uses to hit a baseball.

fans (FANZ) People who watch a sport or game.

home runs (HOME RUNZ) A hit where the batter touches all of the bases and scores a run.

shortstop (SHORT-stop) A position in baseball where the player stands between second and third base.

World Series (WURLD SEER-eez) The games played at the end of the baseball season to decide which team is the best.

Here are more books to read about Derek Jeter and baseball:

Take Me Out to the Ballgame
by Jack Norworth,
Alec Gillman (illustrator)
Aladdin Paperbacks

Derek Jeter: The Yankee Kid
by Jack O'Connell
Sports Publishing, Inc.

To learn more about Derek Jeter and baseball, check out these Web sites:

http://espn.go.com/mlb/profiles/
    profile/5406.html
http://www.majorleaguebaseball.com
http://www.baseballhalloffame.org/

23

Index

Word Count: 108

Note to Librarians, Teachers, and Parents

If reading is a challenge, Reading Power is a solution! Reading Power is perfect for readers who want high-interest subject matter at an accessible reading level. These fact-filled, photo-illustrated books are designed for readers who want straightforward vocabulary, engaging topics, and a manageable reading experience. With clear picture/text correspondence, leveled Reading Power books put the reader in charge. Now readers have the power to get the information they want and the skills they need in a user-friendly format.